WHEN will you understand the PAIN

WHEN *will* *you understand* *the* PAIN

Rev. Tammy Smith D Div.; D Min

 iUniverse®

WHEN WILL YOU UNDERSTAND THE PAIN

Scripture taken from The Holy Bible, King James Version. Public Domain

All scriptures quotes are taken from Bible Gateway, a division of The Zondervan Corporation, 3900 Sparks Drive SE, Grand Rapids, MI 49546 USA. Bible Hub

iUniverse books may be ordered through booksellers or by contacting:

iUniverse
1663 Liberty Drive
Bloomington, IN 47403
www.iuniverse.com
844-349-9409

ISBN: 978-1-6632-1733-2 (sc)
ISBN: 978-1-6632-1734-9 (e)

Print information available on the last page.

iUniverse rev. date: 01/23/2021

Contents

Disclaimer...vii

Dedication ix

Foreword...xi

Preface xiii

Introduction..xv

Chapter 1   What IS mental illness?...1

Chapter 2   Types of mental illness 5

Chapter 3   Who may be at risk? 13

Chapter 4   Take this quiz, Test your knowledge.................................19

Chapter 5   What are some Early Warning Signs We Overlooked?....25

Chapter 6   Statistically Speaking...29

Chapter 7   Does this happen in our churches? YES!!.................................33

Chapter 8   TIME to END the SILENCE 39

Chapter 9   Shore up your mental and emotional health.................41

Chapter 10 Now that we know, what do we do? 47

Chapter 11 That can't happen in my family, I'm (fill in the blank)....53

Chapter 12 About the Author 57

References 71

Disclaimer

Last updated January 15, 2021

The information provided in this book is designed to provide helpful information and resources on the subject of mental illness/health. This book is NOT meant to be used, nor should it be used, to diagnose or treat any medical condition. For diagnosis or treatment PLEASE contact your physician.

This book is for information and educational purposes only, and does not replace professional medical advice, diagnosis or treatment.

The publisher and author are not responsible for any specific health needs that require medical treatment and are/will not be liable for any damage or negative consequences from any actions, to any person reading or following the information in this book. References are provided for information purposes ONLY and do constitute endorsement of any website or sources. Readers should be aware that websites listed in this book are subject to change.

Dedication

This book is dedicated to born again believers who believe God, yet, due to mental health challenges contemplate or complete suicide. This book is to help ease the stigma associated with church goers who have or do entertain suicidal thoughts. This book is dedicated to family members who have mental illness and to the family who has been silent about it for decades, does not have to be silent any more. This book is also to let others know **you're not alone** in this struggle and **there is** a solution, pray to God and talk to a therapist or a counselor, there's nothing wrong with getting **help.**

The information contained in this book is drawn from a variety of sources about mental illness; and is not a comprehensive study. The information is not intended to be used as a diagnostic tool. By reading the contents of this book one is able to identify resources to help address concerns and to contact the resources listed to obtain helpful information. The author cannot endorse everything contained from the listed resources but hopes the information will be useful.

Foreword

A foreword is written by somebody other than the author, and usually tells of some interaction between the writer of the foreword and the author during the writing of the book.

Preface

This book was developed to ensure believers-church goers, whether pastors, evangelists, teachers, ministers, or lay persons, the general public and reader-life happens. Mental illness carries with it stigma that causes individuals to hide real feelings of hopelessness and helplessness. Mental illness is not talked about, preached about, there are no webinars, and is taboo within the church, particularly in the black church.

From the pulpit to the usher at the back door mental illness is not a subject matter discussed. Pray more, fast more "everything will be alright is not always the answer albeit it helps."

Sometimes it is furthest from the truth. You "live right", you help others, faithful to God, family, and the church...so WHY does this happen?"

Introduction

Life's challenges can impact anyone's life at some point or other. Experts say that 1 in 5 people will experience mental illness in their lifetime that can impact their mental health. Do you take ownership of what you feel or do you push those feelings aside or ignore them. Is this a time to "man up", or believe the lie that "big girls don't cry."

Take note: EVERYONE has feelings (emotions). It is part of our humanity, our DNA, it's the way God designed us from the beginning. Allow the words within these pages help you to process your feelings and address them appropriately. There's **no shame** in asking for or seeking help. Most find it advantageous to talk out their feelings with someone they can trust.

However when it involves the religious sector, people "just don't discuss it." The message they tell or portray, "I'm ok, or I'll be ok" masking the pain within. God forbid they are in a leadership role (Pastor, Evangelist, Teacher, Prophet/Prophetess, Elder, Bishop, Reverend).

What one permits to plague their thinking to the point where life to them no longer has any value, can lead to serious consequences possibly death.

How do we deal with mental health in church? I will try to help address this in the upcoming chapters. This question was asked by a former pastor who almost died from suicide.[1]

Intrigued? Please keep reading.

Chapter One

WHAT IS MENTAL ILLNESS?

Let's define mental illness and who may be at risk.

Mental health is our social, emotional, psychological well being.

According to experts (NAMI) *mental health helps to determine how we handle stress, how we interact in our relationship(s) to others, and the type of choices we make.*[2] Mental health is important at every stage of life, childhood, adolescence through adulthood.

The World Health Organization (WHO) defines mental illness on this wise: *mental health is a state of well being in which a person realizes his/her abilities, can cope with "normal stressors" of life, can work productively and fruitfully, and able to make a contribution to his/her community.*[3]

Other factors that have an influence or may contribute to mental health complications include our DNA, or brain chemistry, life experiences, i.e trauma or abuse, family history of mental health illness.

Mental health illness/problems are common. **Anyone** can be affected. Mental illness has NO respect for persons, no one is exempt.

Being educated in regards to mental illness and how it affects one's life and the lives around them is power.

Mental Illness, also called mental health disorder is noted as a wide range of mental health conditions/disorders affecting one's mood, thinking as well as behavior. [4]

Mental illness is a broad range of medical conditions (i.e. major depression, schizophrenia, obsessive compulsive disorder, or panic disorder) marked primarily by sufficient disorganization of personality, mind, or emotions that impair normal psychological functioning causing marked distress, disability and is typically associated with a disruption in normal thinking, feeling, mood, behavior, interpersonal interactions, or daily functioning [5]

Mental illness, to the general public (churches, schools, daycares, persons served, just to name a few) goes unnoticed or may be seen as "he/she is having a bad day", is exhausted, overworked, is "off", not themselves, etc. Note not everyone "having a bad day" has a mental illness. They could be having a bad day, however when those "bad days," feeling out of control, feelings of hopelessness, helpless, that seem to continue over an extended period of time without end, may be an indication that a problem exists and may need addressed.

Where to start, share this with your family, clergy, make an appointment with your PCP, talk openly with your PCP. Share what you feel, how long you have been feeling that way. Ask for their recommendations then get help.

BEFORE you begin consuming their recommended anxiety medication, ask for a referral and share with a professional, YES, a psychiatrist, he/she can diagnose the problem and then make recommendations.

When feeling out of sorts does not mean one has a mental illness. This book is not developed for individuals to self diagnose.This book is a resource to help its readers to be informed, educated, and able to help someone who may be struggling with symptoms, getting them the help they need.

Everyone experiences ups and downs with mental health. Stressful experiences may include loss of a loved one, witnessing a violent act against a loved one, a victim of a heinous crime against their person just to name a few. These occurences might temporarily diminish one's psychological well-being. Generally, in order to meet the criteria for mental illness, symptoms must cause significant distress or interfere with an individual's social, occupational, or educational functioning and last for a defined period of time.

Some common signs of mental illness in adults and adolescents can include:[6]

- **Changes in sleep or appetite**: Sleeping and eating habits have dramatically change more or less than usual, noticeable and rapid weight gain or loss
- **Mood changes**: Extreme sadness, inability to express joy, indifference to situations, feelings of hopelessness, laughter at inappropriate times for no apparent reason, or thoughts of suicide.
- **Withdrawal**: Sitting and doing nothing for long periods of time or abandon previously enjoyed activities
- **Problems thinking**: Inability to concentrate or problems with memory or logical thoughts and speech which is explain
- **Excessive fear or uneasiness**: Feeling afraid, anxious, nervous, or panicked

Please note, experiencing 1 or 2 symptoms does not necessarily mean you have a mental illness, however it may indicate the necessity of a psychological evaluation. Should one be experiencing several symptoms at the same time and have difficulty functioning in a daily routine may need to consult with one's PCP or a mental health professional.

Mental health illnesses may not be curable however it is treatable and a person can, depending on the individual diagnosis, the severity of your symptoms, and results, can be managed through various therapies i.e. medication management, talk therapy or both.

Chapter Two

TYPES OF MENTAL ILLNESS

Some of these illnesses (bolded) are common, i.e. **depression** and **anxiety**, anxiety disorders, including panic disorder, obsessive-compulsive disorder, and phobias, depression, bipolar disorder, and other mood disorders.

Eating disorders. Personality disorders. Post-traumatic stress disorder.

Personality disorders.

Post-traumatic stress disorder.

Psychotic disorders, including schizophrenia

Two of the most common disorders highlighted above will be defined.

Defining depression: *Depression known as major depressive disorder is a common yet a serious medical illness negatively affecting how one feels, thinks and acts. It is treatable. Depression causes feelings of sadness, a loss of interest in activities once enjoyed. It can lead to various emotional and physical problems decreasing a person's ability to function at work and at home.*[1]

Other experts say that *depression-a mood disorder causes a persistent feeling of sadness and loss of interest. Also called major depressive disorder or clinical depression, affecting how one feels, thinks and behaves, leading to various emotional and physical problems. People affected by depression may have trouble doing normal day-to-day activities, and sometimes may make one feel as if life isn't worth living.*[2]

SYMPTOMS

In order to receive a diagnosis of depression, symptoms must persist for more than two weeks. Symptoms can vary from mild to severe there are some other medical conditions i.e. thyroid problems, a brain tumor or vitamin deficiency) that can mimic symptoms of depression. It is imperative to have a professional rule out general medical causes. Those depressive symptom include but not limited to:

- Feelings of sadness or a depressed mood
- Loss of interest or pleasure in activities once enjoyed
- Changes in appetite — weight loss or gain unrelated to dieting
- Trouble sleeping or sleeping too much
- Loss of energy or increased fatigue
- Increase in purposeless physical activity (e.g., hand-wringing or pacing) or slowed movements and speech (actions observable by others)
- Feeling worthless or guilty
- Difficulty thinking, concentrating or making decisions
- Thoughts of death or suicide

Note being sad because of the death of a loved one, termination of a relationship and bouts of sadness may not necessarily be depression.

People suffering from depression may report feeling as if they've lost the ability to visualize a happy future, nor remember a happy past. They don't realize although they're suffering from a treatable illness, seeking help may not even enter their mind. Emotions and physical pain become unbearable. Not wanting to die, they feel as though it's the only way their pain will end.

Depressed? This test may indicate the possibility, however **it is only a tool** to help make an individual aware that seeking a mental health professional may be advantageous. It is **not** to be used as diagnosis for depression or any other mental illness.

For the last 2 weeks, how often have you been bothered by any of the following problems?

1. Little interest or pleasure in doing things

- Not at all
- Several days
- More than half the days
- Nearly every day

2. Feeling down, depressed, or hopeless

- Not at all
- Several days
- More than half the days
- Nearly every day

3. Trouble falling or staying asleep, or sleeping too much

- Not at all
- Several days
- More than half the days
- Nearly every day

4. Feeling tired or having little energy

- Not at all
- Several days
- More than half the days
- Nearly every day

5. Poor appetite or overeating

- Not at all
- Several days
- More than half the days
- Nearly every day

6. Feeling bad about yourself - or that you are a failure or have let yourself or your family down

- Not at all
- Several days
- More than half the days
- Nearly every day

7. Trouble concentrating on things, such as reading the newspaper or watching television

- Not at all
- Several days
- More than half the days
- Nearly every day

8. Moving or speaking so slowly that other people could have noticed

Or the opposite - being so fidgety or restless that you have been moving around a lot more than usual

- Not at all
- Several days
- More than half the days
- Nearly every day

9. Thoughts that you would be better off dead, or of hurting yourself

- Not at all
- Several days
- More than half the days
- Nearly every day

10. If you checked off any problems, how difficult have these problems made it for you at work, home, or with other people?

- Not difficult at all
- Somewhat difficult
- Very difficult
- Extremely difficult

Other questions asked would be statical information identifying age, gender, race, income, any previous diagnosis of mental illness, previous treatment for mental illness, contributing factors that may lead to depression, what group affiliation i.e. veteran, trauma survivor, gender affiliation, occupation, recent changes finances etc or any pre-existing health conditions. If you think what you are experiencing may be depression, confer with your physician. It's a start.

Define anxiety: It is how your body naturally responds to stress. It's a feeling of fear (false evidence appearing real) or apprehension about what may come. Anxiety can cause significant worry about issues such as your future. Anxiety is an increase of **stress.** It is any big event or an accumulation of smaller stressful life situations that may trigger excessive anxiety.

One major anxiety disorder is generalized anxiety disorder (GAD). Those experiencing GAD may have the symptoms listed below.

Feeling restless, wound-up, or on-edge· Easily fatigued. Difficulty concentrating; mind going blank. Irritable Intense worry about many things i.e. personal, work, relationships, life in general for a period of 6 months or more is defined as general anxiety disorder.[3]

Generalized anxiety disorder (GAD) symptoms may include:

- Feeling restless, wound-up, or on-edge
- Easily fatigued
- Difficulty concentrating; the mind going blank
- Irritable
- Muscle tension
- Difficulty controlling feelings of worry
- Sleep problems, i.e. difficulty falling or staying asleep, restlessness, or unsatisfying sleep.

Sure at times we can get overly concerned about life's challenges, health, money, job status, relationships etc. It's what we do. Some people, when anxiety is constant and excessive in nature over everyday life situations for an extended period of time may cause an individual to avoid responsibilities i.e. like going to work, school, family gatherings etc worsening symptoms leading to health conditions, substance use and the like.

With generalized anxiety disorder (GAD), people become extremely worried or nervous about these and other things—sometimes there is little or no reason to worry about them. Individuals with GAD have a difficult time controlling their anxiety and staying focused on daily responsibilities. Read (Phillipians 4:8; Isaiah 26:3; John 14:27; 2 Timothy 1:7; Philippians 4:6-7

Short story: May 60+ year old woman, has a crippling disease. Her infamous words are "I worry", or "it makes me nervous" … "what if", consistently. The distorted thinking has resulted in other symptoms surfacing in addition to the incurable malady she deals with on a day to day basis. May refuses to go outside of the confines of the home fearful and will justify her feelings with a "what if."

May finally admitted she may be suffering from depression. May professes to be a believer-a christian. She is not alone in this struggle, and she is willing to seek help. No more secrecy. Soon she will be free to live a productive, happy, fulfilled life. First Step...talk to her PCP (primary care physician) about her worries, her PCP will refer her to a specialist/counselor who can better help May with depression and anxiety.

Because of COVID-19 telehealth (talk therapy) is as sufficient as face to face (clinical) therapy. This platform has many pros...flexible schedule, limits travel to an office, can be accomplished in the comfort of one's home. This is only one method of treatment. There are several others and the participant can choose the best form of mental help for them.

What are some other treatment options? Besides psychotherapy, there is medication,and or a combination of both. It also helps to educate yourself about depression and or anxiety, not to self diagnose however to become aware of what the mental illness is and the treatments available, to help minimize symptoms, identify there are no underlying medical issues, to live a productive life. Involvement in a support group and avoid isolation. You can make it...you are not alone.

Chapter Three

WHO MAY BE AT RISK?

Individuals whose attributes demonstrate the inability to manage one's thoughts, emotions, behaviours and interactions with others, including social, cultural, economic, political and environmental factors such as national policies, social protection, standards of living, working conditions, and community support.

Stress, genetics, nutrition, perinatal infections and exposure to environmental hazards are also contributing factors to mental illness/disorders [1]

Notice the words "**inability to manage** (losing one's ability to control) thoughts, emotions, behaviors, their interactions with others which includes every aspect and area that has an impact on how we respond to our surroundings. When that ceases to exist there is a problem.

This can affect any individual including believers, those who are affiliated with church.

This concern had surfaced recently in 2018 however since this pandemic COVID-19 it is resurfacing again. As from the very beginning "the church" is still silent around this topic either from lack of information, not sure how to address it, and denial.

Isaiah 26:3 *"Thou wilt keep him in perfect peace, whose mind is stayed on thee: because he trusteth in thee."* (biblegateway)

Undeniable God can and will, consider this, not everyone who attends church (your church) has been saved all their lives. New comers, old timers, may have been able to manage their thoughts, emotions until life happens.

When life happens and unplanned life changing events happen (i.e. stress, job loss, loss of loved one, financial woes, distress, chaos in the community, home environment etc.) can be responsible for the manifestation of mental illness causing the individual's inability to manage their thoughts, emotions, behaviors and interactions with others. Needless to say sin may not have been the blame. Sadly the church has not given much grace to mental illness or to those it affects.

{True story} Name has been changed to protect the innocent. Mother (Adelyne) with 8 children and no means of transportation, needed to go to the store around 6 pm Saturday evening for milk, cereal, and pampers. Adelyne made a poor choice in leaving her 8 children home alone, the oldest being 10. Her thought was she could get to the store quicker without taking all her kids with her to the store which was a few blocks away. The neighbor noticed the mom had left and did not see the children accompanying her which they normally did.

The neighbor took it upon themself to call the police. Police arrived at the home, mom had been gone for 15 minutes. Oldest child opens the door, and the police enter an unkempt but clean home. Kids had toys, clothes, all over the house, opened food containers etc on the table. Officer asks where the mom/adults were.

Oldest states he did not know. Officer asks how long she had been gone. Again the oldest states "I don't know."

Police made the decision to gather the children, took them to a nearby hospital and notified CYS. Adelyne returns home and discovers all of her children are gone. She frantically scours the neighborhood calling her children by name. A neighbor hears her calling and comes out to her aid. The neighbor informs the mother that the police were seen placing her children in vehicles and taking them away.

Adelyne calls the police and shows up at the station only to be told her children were in the custody of CYS. Adelyne contacted the CYS night intake worker. Per the worker the report had not come in yet and she would be contacted as soon as possible. Adelyne was unable to eat or sleep for several days not knowing where her children were if they were safe and not getting direct information from the workers.

That Monday she received notification that her children had been placed in emergency foster care, there would be a hearing in a few days for which she would need to attend. Court day, decision passed, to this Adelyne's dismay, her children will remain in care.

Adelyne lost her children, lost her income (welfare), the landlord evicted her, she had been moving from place to place, unable to see the children at scheduled visits with no money or transportation to get to the CYS office.

With no hope of ever seeing her children, minimal family or community support Adelyne had a mental break. With no health insurance, no monetary funds, homeless, with only the clothes on her back, no job skills Adelyne, when around family members began displaying unusual behaviors. She would be seen pacing and talking to herself, literally would jump as if startled by something or someone. Her behavior became so bizarre that her family members no longer welcomed her in their homes for fear that she may harm them.

Having to live on the street and sleeping where and when she could, Adelyne wandered around the city begging for money to eat. Carrying a bag of clothes given to her from the last shelter she visited. She could be seen talking to an individual or someone and was often heard by passers by talking to her children who were no longer there.

Many signs were visible, change in personal care (wearing several layered articles of clothing) moods fluctuated from sadness to heightened excitability/gaiety, limited logical thinking, and unusual behavior. To her demise she was unaware of what was happening to her and could not explain her behavior. To Adelyne's demise she had no insurance and lacked medical help/intervention.

It so happened that on a particular Sunday Adelyne happened past a church. Upon entering, visibly she appeared "normal" except for her physical appearance.

She refused to be escorted to a seat and meandered down the aisle to find her a seat of her choosing. While seated Adelyne jumped up from her seat and looked around as if startled by a sudden noise/sound. She began talking to an invisible person sitting next to her. This behavior made the people sitting on the same pew get up and moved to the other side of the church. Adelyne got up, looked at several people nodded to them then sat in a different pew. This behavior continued during the church service.

An usher came close and asked if she needed anything, Adelyne got up and moved to the other side of the sanctuary. The minister continued the sermon as if nothing was transpiring.

Several church members attempted to usher her out but with much resistance and beginning to settle she was permitted to remain until the end of service. Adelyne was offered prayer for which she accepted, yet afterward left unchanged in behavior.

Several church members passed by her, some snickering and gawking at her. A member asked if she needed a ride to somewhere, she accepted.

A conversation which Adelyne revealed her despairing past which explained her outlandish behavior.

Because one individual showed empathy toward Adelyne, she continued to attend Sunday services periodically. Adelyne's behavior began to deteriorate as time progressed.

To Adelyne her only hope for healing was in church, however misunderstandings, fear, being uninformed, and believing mental illness was God's way of punishing that sinful person, the Church made it difficult for Adelyne struggling with mental illness to find the help she desperately needed. Adelyne did not recover, did not get her children back, did not receive the love and support from her family or the church.

WHAT could have, or what can the church do now to help those who may be struggling with mental illness? One important step for churches is to talk about mental health struggles in a compassionate and **informed** way.

This will help people in your congregation understand what mental illnesses are and how to better offer support to those who are struggling to find help within their church and or in their community. Mental illness like physical illnesses may not be cured, however with information and the church's support, people with mental illness can learn to live with the illness and learn to draw closer to God in the midst of it all.

What are some mental illnesses your congregants are struggling with? PTSD (veterans) We honor them for serving but can one identify the signs and symptoms? You may not be trained in the area to address the symptoms however, having the resources available to help is a start. Are you aware of the resources available? Is there a support group addressing the issues? What is being done to "equip the saints for the work of the ministry in your church?"

Chapter Four

TAKE THIS QUIZ, TEST
YOUR KNOWLEDGE

1. A colleague, perhaps a congregant, family member, close friend whom you have known for many,many years was a victim of a violent, physical assault. Having been diagnosed with anxiety disorder breaks down, sweating profusely, while doubling over in pain and now is hyperventilating. What do you do?

    a. Move this person to a quiet place, get them him/her to slow their breathing.

    b. Give the person time alone because attention to this situation will encourage repetitive behaviors.

    c. Take the person somewhere for tea, coffee, or something to calm them down,pointing out that the attacker is nowhere to be found and their emotions are getting the best of them.

2. You've noticed that a family member, a sophomore in college, has has not been functioning well as the year Progresses. First semester he/she was doing quite well, and seemed to enjoy all their classes. Now, there has been noticeable weight loss, seems depressed, lacking focus no motivation, and when having a conversation with them they express peculiar things. Do you:

   a. Tell him/her that they need substance abuse treatment and you are sorry they have fallen prey to common college issues like drinking and drugs.
   b. Suggest they consult with their academic counselor or get a tutor to get back on track.
   c. Express your concern and offer to help refer them to on campus counseling or other services

3. Back in your college days, your friend use to use recreational marijuana regularly accompanied by a few social drinks. Now on visits to the home you've noticed a familiar smell and their behavior appears off and there is a significant personality Change. What do you do?

   a. Say what your concern is regarding their noticeable change behavior. Ask them to talk to you about those changes.
   b. Tell them to stop drinking because the bible says:....drinking is a sin and even though marijuana is a natural substance they shouldn't do it and quote more bible.
   c. Say they have a drug problem and you won't associate yourself with them until they get it together.

4. You are picking up your child/grandchild, or a neighbor's children from school, and notice an adult's behavior is strange. This individual is walking around having a heated discussion with an invisible person. Do You:

WHEN will you understand the PAIN

a. Ignore them/not your problem, as long as he/she doesn't approach you.

b. Assess the situation as to whether there is any imminent risk to you or others. Encourage any onlookers to not confront this individual. If you feel safe approach them in a non threatening way, asking if they are ok and what help do they need. Notify school officials.

c. Approach the individual, standing right in front of them, giving them direct eye contact, putting your hands on their shoulder, telling them they need to leave the premise

5. You are concerned about a coworker (colleague, congregant, best friend) who had been difficult lately. His/her work has not been up to par and often missed deadlines. He/she has frequently called out sick seeming to ok the day before. The night before at a gathering, where they are usually the life of the party was exceptionally quiet and preferred drinking alone. You get a call and this individual states he/she can't take the pressure and are considering resigning. What do you do?

a. Tell him/her you are aware of the frequent call off, missed deadlines and have been unapproachable regarding the other employees.

b. Tell him/her you are concerned and ask if they can better clarify the pressure he/she is feeling.

c. Say based on what you have seen during social gatherings drinking is not an option.

6. You're at home watching your favorite movie when a frantic call from a colleague threatening suicide. Do you:

a. End the call quickly, not your concern. You learned that people who threaten suicide rarely go through it. They'll calm down sooner or later and be ok.

21

    b. You ask if they have a plan or have made any previous attempts or have considered what resources to use to complete suicide now. Have a conversation with them about staying safe, calling the 1-800-273-8255 or seeking professional help.

    c. Ask how he/she intends to kill him/herself. If they don't have a plan he/she is probably not serious and you can go back to enjoying your movie.

7. A colleague (congregant,) has lost all their self-image in his/her appearance and zeal for life. Speech is wearisome, he/she is sad all the time,and recently has began giving their most valuable possessions. What do you do?

    a. Ask if there is anything they would like to talk about, ask if they are depressed, if so how long,and have they had any thoughts about ending their life.

    b. Keep the conversation light by avoiding any discussion of suiside or death because he/she is upset enough and you want to avoid putting the thought into their head.

    c. Take them out for ice cream or wine, coffee, latte, or an espresso because caffeine will help them snap out of it.

8. Your at a gathering and one of the members becomes violent. He/she has a knife, it appears he/she is responding to voices that are in his/her head. Do you:

    a. Pretend to hear voices too in order to gain trust and to be able to take the knife away.

    b. Take him/her down physically by any means necessary.

    c. Call 911 and while awaiting police presence quiet whatever is going on as well as the people, ensure a clear exit and possible have someone calmly speak to the individual avoiding any quarreling

9. You and your neighbor get along quite well, however the loud music and frequent guests are disturbing. This neighbor and frequent mood fluctuations seems to be able to stay awake endlessly and thinks the neighborhood should too. There are times when she may not come out of her house or say hello. Do you:

    a. Try and catch her when she seems to be having a better day and share your concerns about her mood swings and suggest she talk to her physician offering to accompany her if need be.
    b. Keep your distance because her split personality tire you both.
    c. Be direct with her despicable behavior and confront her about her obvious mental illness.

10. It's the holidays one of your family members has appeared emaciated. They say they have been working on a project and often take food up to their room however when you check on them the food is untouched. What do you say?

    a. Compliment them on self control during a time when everyone else is gorging on food-saying keep up the good work.
    b. Engage your family member in a conversation asking how are things going for them and ask if there is anything they want to talk about.
    c. You leave them alone because they usually seem ok.

How did you do in answering these questions? Will you have any discomfort in being able to talk to someone about what may be a problem?

It can be difficult to talk to a person about what may be going on with them. If they are resistant, or not willing to talk about it, let the individual know when they want to talk you are there for them.

Rev. Tammy Smith D Div.; D Min

Begin a support group at your local assembly/church, have trained professionals come to your church, talk about mental illnesses, signs and symptoms to become aware of and how you may help.

Gather resourceful information to give to those who may be suffering and where they can turn for help spiritually, emotionally, and mentally.

As always praying for them and being there as a support is key. No one struggling with mental illness needs shunned or made to feel as though they should find another place of worship, or not welcomed in the house of God.

The Spirit of the Lord God is upon me; because the Lord hath anointed me to preach good tidings unto the meek; he hath sent me to bind up the brokenhearted, to proclaim liberty to the captives, and the opening of the prison to them that are bound;

2 To proclaim the acceptable year of the Lord, and the day of vengeance of our God; to comfort all that mourn;

3 To appoint unto them that mourn in Zion, to give unto them beauty for ashes, the oil of joy for mourning, the garment of praise for the spirit of heaviness; that they might be called trees of righteousness, the planting of the Lord, that he might be glorified **Isaiah 61:1-3**

Luke 4:18 *The Spirit of the Lord is upon me, because he hath anointed me to preach the gospel to the poor; he hath sent me to heal the brokenhearted, to preach deliverance to the captives, and recovering of sight to the blind, to set at liberty them that are bruised,*

Resources:
(**NAMI**, 2-1-1, 1-800-273-TALK) (8255)
The Center • **A Place of HOPE 1-888-771-5166 / 425-771-5166**
Grace Wellness Center (724) 863-7223 Monroeville, Pa, US 15146

Chapter Five

WHAT ARE SOME EARLY WARNING SIGNS WE OVERLOOKED?

Identifying the warning signs early on what may lead to mental illness or that a problem may exist.

- Eating or sleeping too much or too little
- Isolating from people and their usual activities
- Exhibiting low or no energy
- Feeling numb or like nothing matters
- Unexplained body aches and pains
- Feeling helpless or hopeless
- Smoking, drinking, drug use or abuse more than usual
- Feeling confused, seemingly forgetful, edgy, angry, upset, worried, or scared
- Yelling or fighting with family and friends
- Severe mood swings causing problems in relationships

- Persistent thoughts and memories that seem to stick in your head
- Hearing voices or believing things that are not true
- Thinking of harming yourself or others
- Inability to perform daily tasks like taking care of your kids or getting to work, school or ministerial duties.

So, why do we neglect or fail to notice these pertinent symptoms? What excuse or rationalization do we desperately cling to when we see a loved one, friend, colleague, or congregant who may have experienced several of the symptoms mentioned above? What doubt, uncertainty or ambivalence causes us to dissociate those symptoms with the individual in question?

We honestly do not want to believe it could possibly happen to a christian, someone who seems strong in the faith, consistently believes in God the creator of the universe.

What do we do with these scriptures (Job 14:1, 22; Isaiah 38:1-3; Romans 8:18, 2 Corinthians 4: 8, 9; 17; 1 Peter 4:12,)

Job 1:1, 14:1, 22 1 *There was a man in the land of Uz, whose name was Job; and that man was* **perfect and upright***, and one that* **feared God***, and eschewed evil.*

14 *Man that is born of a woman is of few days and full of trouble.* **22** *But his flesh upon him shall have* **pain***, and his soul within him shall mourn.*

Isaiah 38:1-3 *In those days was Hezekiah* **sick unto death***.* **2** *Then Hezekiah turned his face toward the wall, and prayed unto the Lord,* **3** *And said, Remember now, O Lord, I beseech thee, how I have* **walked before thee in truth and with a perfect heart***, and have done that which is good in thy sight. And Hezekiah wept sore.*

Romans 8:18 *For I reckon that the* **sufferings** *of this present time are not worthy to be compared with the glory which shall be revealed in us.*

2 Corinthians 4:8, 9; 17 *We are **troubled** on every side, yet not distressed; we are perplexed, but not in despair;*

9 *Persecuted, but not forsaken; cast down, but not destroyed;* **17** *For our light affliction, which is but for a moment, worketh for us a far more exceeding and eternal weight of glory;*

1Peter 4:12 *Beloved, think it not strange concerning the **fiery trial** which is to try you, as though some strange thing happened unto you*

Chapter Six

STATISTICALLY SPEAKING

1 in 5 U.S. adults experience mental illness each year

- 1 in 25 U.S. adults experience serious mental illness each year
- 1 in 6 U.S. youth aged 6-17 experience a mental health disorder each year
- 50% of all lifetime mental illness begins by age 14, and 75% by age 24
- Some realize they have a problem and get help, UNFORTUNATELY others are afraid of the stigma, ashamed, fearful of what others may think and say, and won't get the **help** that's **available**.

Let's talk about suicide, it's ok to talk about it, and it should be a topic of discussion especially in the church.

- Suicide is the 2nd leading cause of death among people aged 10-34 in the U.S.
- Suicide is the 10th leading cause of death in the U.S.
- The overall suicide rate in the U.S. has increased by 31% since 2001
- 46% of people who die by suicide had a diagnosed mental health condition
- 90% of people who die by suicide had shown symptoms of a mental health condition, according to interviews with family, friends and medical professionals.

Due to the pandemic COVID-19, people having to shelter in place and due to the CDC guidelines, loss of lives, loss of jobs, scarcity of the essentials needed to thrive, and all the other things we are now encountering, the statistics of mental illness and suicide may increase in number.

Taking first steps can be confusing and frightening but knowing **you are not alone** and **your life matters** is all the more reason to seek professional help now.

More statistics: mental illness among U.S. adults, by demographic group:

Non-Hispanic Asian: 14.7%
Non-Hispanic white: 20.4%
Non-Hispanic black: 16.2%
  Non-Hispanic American Indian or Alaska Native: 22.1%
  Non-Hispanic mixed/multiracial: 26.8%
  Hispanic or Latino: 16.9%
  Lesbian, Gay or Bisexual: 37.4% 3

According to Massachusstes chief physiatrist Dr. Maurizio Fava, an increase in mental illness, in conjunction with pandemic COVID-19 is not surprising.

He goes on to say that the increase in depression due to the pandemic is based on people's fear of contracting the disease, grief from the loss of loved ones, job loss, unemployment, loss of housing, lack of access to caregivers, inability to interact within the community, not having physical access to primary care physicians, "unprecedented social distancing" (something we not accustomed to) unable to attend church services, etc.[1].

Chapter Seven

DOES THIS HAPPEN IN OUR CHURCHES? YES!!

One individual (former pastor) shared "I longed for death **feeling hopeless."** [1]

Ask yourself, were there warning signs regarding Sis/Brother So & So? What were those signs?

Be not deceived, mental illness **does** happen, and it DOES happen to believers in the church.

We cannot overlook the fact that ***our "adversary the devil"*** *prowls around like a roaring lion, seeking someone to devour"* (1 Pet. 5:8 NIV).

Time magazine writes: Sept. 11, 2019 California megachurch pastor frequently spoke out on the issues of mental health sharing his own struggles with **depression** died on Monday by suicide at the age of 30.

Jarrid Wilson joined the Harvest Christian Fellowship church in Riverside, Calif. 18 months ago as an associate pastor, according to a statement from the church. The church has a congregation of 15,000.

"He was vibrant, positive, and was always serving and helping others," the statement said. "He wanted to especially help those who were dealing with suicidal thoughts."

"Sometimes people may think that as pastors or spiritual leaders we are somehow above the pain and struggles of everyday people," the church's senior pastor Greg Laurie wrote in a blog post mourning Wilson's death that Tuesday. "We are the ones who are supposed to have all the answers. But we do not."

Jarrid is survived by his wife Julianne and two sons. Julianne shared an emotional tribute on Instagram, writing that her husband was a "loving, giving, kind-hearted, encouraging, handsome, hilarious, give the shirt [off] his back husband."

"No more pain, my Jerry, no more struggle. You are made complete and you are finally free. Suicide and **depression fed you** the worst **lies,** but **you knew the truth of Jesus** and I know you're by his side right this very second," was what her post read.

Wilson and his wife were the founders of an outreach program called "Anthem of Hope," which set out to help people dealing with depression and suicidal thoughts.

In a 2017 podcast interview with ChurchLeaders.com, Wilson cited the Bible's Book of Job, arguing that "Some of God's brightest saints dealt with the darkest of depression. What we have to understand is that just because you're dealing with depression or suicidal thoughts does not mean you're any less of a believer or a Christian than anybody else."

And in a column written a year later for the site, he wrestled further with scriptural precedent and the *stigma* many place upon suicide and suicidal thoughts or ideation. Such judgments, Harris wrote, "ill-thought and without proper biblical understanding... [they] obviously don't understand the totality of mental health issues in today's world, let alone understand the basic theology behind compassion and God's all-consuming grace."

- He continued: Does God approve of suicide? No!
- Does God view suicide as a bad thing? Yes!
- Is God's grace sufficient even for those who have committed suicide? Yes!

The day before his death, Wilson tweeted that faith couldn't always be seen as a "cure" but added that it "doesn't mean Jesus doesn't offer us companionship and comfort. He ALWAYS does that."[2]

If you or someone you know may be contemplating suicide, call the **National Suicide Prevention Lifeline at 1-800-273-8255** or text HOME to 741741 to reach the Crisis Text Line. In emergencies, call 911, or **seek care** from a local hospital or mental health provider.

How can one understand this shocking tragedy?

As mentioned earlier the scripture is this: ...because your adversary the devil, as a roaring lion, walketh about (prowls around), seeking (someone)whom he may devour: (1 Peter 5: 8b)

There are several accounts in scripture where kings,

Well renowned Bishop/Overseer (name not permitted to publish) holding 2 doctorate degrees, struggled 3 ½ years with depression and anxiety, shares the story of overcoming **depression**, fear, and anxiety; discovering the path to personal wholeness; and finding peace in the midst of life's storms ....

This pastor states the journey was "a time of prolonged intense testing" calling it the "perfect storm" and references Job 3:25 (Job experiencing severe anxiety) *For the thing which I greatly feared is come upon me, and that which I was afraid of is come unto me.*

Apostle Paul tells us in Phillipians 4:6, 7 *Be careful for nothing; but in every thing by prayer and supplication with thanksgiving let your requests be made known unto God. And the peace of God, which passeth all understanding, shall keep your hearts and minds through Christ Jesus.* (KJV) bible gateway. Yet Paul himself endured intense fear and anxiety *And I was with you in weakness, and in fear, and in much trembling.* (1 Corinthians 2:3 KJV)bible gateway

Some believers are indeed suffering in silence, the *fear* and the stigma causing them to embrace the "what if" stinkin thinkin which breeds fear, anxiety and depression. Time to take the masks off, be freed from the darkness of the soul, and seek help. Want peace, get help, be free.

I have asked that pastors from various areas including the state where this author resided, that they anonymously indicate if they have experienced any of their congregants diagnosed with mental health conditions, or are they equipped to help families whose loved ones have attempted or have completed suicide. If so, what resources do they have in place to assist those families. Not one responded.

I also reviewed an article from a young woman who agrees with my view that "the church needs to become a **valuable resource** for those who struggle with mental health conditions", and realize it is not a lack of faith when an individual struggles with mental illness. That the church would also become and continue to become a place of healing as it once was. There are some "clergy" not willing to be transparent with their own struggles, they just take sabbaticals or they choose to cover up their struggles and put their "I'm blessed and highly favored" mask on while inwardly they are pained emotionally.

It's when the inward pain makes a grand entrance as migraines, high blood pressure, stroke, aneurysms, anxiety, depression and other mental health problems that the truth comes out.

Another tragic account

Ellen was a faithful church goer. She would call for the van to be picked up for church. Often than most she would bring her favorite instrument(s) to play (so she thought), you see Ellen could not play a note.To her what she played was music to her ears.To everyone else a complete racket. Ellen could be described as cheerful, very loving, easy, loyal going and dedicated by temperament. Ellen would give you the clothes off her back if she thought you needed them.

If professionally descriptive and categorized her personality traits, she would fall under the Supine Temperament. Ellen had difficulty expressing herself. In a spiritual sense she esteemed others more highly than herself.(*"Let nothing be done through strife or vainglory; but in lowliness of mind let each esteem other better than themselves."*) Philipians 2:3 KJV-bible hub

Ellen stayed mainly to herself, she had a gentle spirit, always willing to serve if she understood what was expected of her. Ellen displayed a great desire to serve others, yone could depend of Ellen, she was loyal to the ministry she associated with, and when anyone she responded to ask her about christianity she would state she could feel God's love, joy, and peace.Ellen also responded to genuine love from others but as usual her church affiliation had no understanding of mental or physical abnormalities and accounted her actions as demonic.

One of the pastors would grab her head and spout "in the name of Jesus-loose her." Ellen would appear bewildered not understanding why her head was grabbed and why this person praying for her would mutter christanese gargan.

Outwardly she appeared quote unquote normal-however Ellen had a problem. Ellen had epilepsy. When Ellen was experiencing a seizure she would cry out or make some sound, stiffen for several minutes, have rhythmic movements of her arms and legs. Her eyes would be open and most of the time. Ellen would pick at her clothes, her body or smack her lips. If she was sitting she would slide off of whatever she was sitting on and fall to the ground. Should she be standing she would throw her head back and hit the ground. The seizures happened quite frequently in church and each time she would be met with the same response. If one person responded to her in a caring manner Ellen would gravitate toward that individual. However if the individual was not able to assist her the usual would happen laying on of hands and attempting to cast out a demon. Once on a bus trip one of the members slapped her and ordered her to stop. Not only was Ellen shocked but many of the church members were stunned as to what had happened.

Ellen may have been prescribed medication however she may not have been taking the medication or forgot to take it prior to coming to church. Her frequent seizure caused many of the church members to be fearful and would either distance themselves from her or would shout at her in hopes she would "snap" out of it. Then it happened. Ellen as she normally would, called for transportation to attend a service. For whatever reason the van was late that day. Ellen had a seizure while waiting outside of her home falling to the ground hitting her head on the concrete. Her head was seriously injured-the van arrived called an ambulance. Ellen had been unresponsive and later that evening the attempts of the attending physicians proved unsuccessful. Had the ministers of her church been informed of Ellen's condition and how to properly respond the outcome may have been different.

Chapter Eight
TIME TO END THE SILENCE

This caption caught my attention. It speaks volumes, and most times we are encouraged to believe that there is *truth* in this statement. "*Black people* don't see therapists. Just *go to church*, and you will be fine. Suicide is a white persons disease."

Mental illness (disorder) may increase the risk of suicide.
Mental illnesses (disorders) having many symptoms affect individuals physically, emotionally, and socially, one's occupation and interpersonal relationships. This mental illness, one that's common, namely depression, is treat-a-ble, however many people suffer from it and are unaware of the symptoms and that they are suffering from it.[1]

What can your church do?

Most are not sure what to do making it difficult to talk about openly.

Many have minimal if any information and knowledge of what mental illness is, have no information about mental illness and if they suspect someone in their congregation is suffering from it, are not comfortable speaking to them. Worse yet those dealing with mental illness are afraid to talk about their concerns because of the fear of being ostracized by the church. Their distorted thinking may cause them to assume they may be demonic oppressed, have sinned (Genesis 4:7), some feeling like a social outcast and may isolate. Where, out of sheer desperation, do individuals turn when experiencing mental illness? They come or call for the church's help (James 5:14-16). Mental illness, like physical illness, needs to be addressed.

It is the **church's** responsibility to minister to the whole individual, body, mind, spirit or is it? To start,

- recognize mental illness does exist, it can happen to anyone.
- Be informed, identify resources that help educate what signs and symptoms of mental illness looks like. It's not always the devil.
- Begin by developing a ministry to help address mental illness.

The church has many ministries, children's ministry, mime ministry, prison ministry, benevolent ministry, outreach ministry, music ministry, hospitality ministry, what is missing in many churches is the **ministry** addressing mental illness. Many churches are unaware of mental health resources that the church can refer those struggling with mental illness to for help.

Identify who in your congregation has counseling background, are licensed/non licensed therapists who have therapeutic experience. Encourage additional training and or education for those identified to carry out that part of ministry.

Chapter Nine

SHORE UP YOUR MENTAL AND EMOTIONAL HEALTH

We are in a crisis, an invisible enemy that has gained control over what we once called "normal existence." COVID-19/Coronavirus has plagued our world, have annihilated lives, ravaged cities, weakened the economy, shut down businesses, closed schools and closed the doors to our churches.

We have become its captives and now we are required to shelter in, avoid going anywhere useless necessary, unless you are considered essential workers. This invisible enemy has enraged people, created what seems to be an unconquerable fear in people. This enemy has produced stress and anxiety because there are no concrete answers as to what is happening, why it's happening, where it came from and who's responsible.

Because of this fear people have raced to get, in a desperate rage, fought over toilet paper, paper towels, hand soap, hand sanitizer, clorox and other "essential" products until the stores were unable to meet supply and demand.

What has gone unnoticed early on was the mental anguish people began to experience being isolated from humanity. Emotions began to run rampant in homes, spouses against spouses, parents against children, siblings against siblings. Parents began to report that little "Jonnie, and little Susie had frequent uncontrollable outbursts of anger, spoke hurtful words, and broke things from fits of rage. Reports of individuals experiencing stress, anxiety, depression in a state of panic, some seeking help from others reacting to what they don't understand.

Husbands became verbally abusive, often physically abusive (as reported by the media). Nobody saw this coming. There has arisen Unchecked emotions due to the inability to address mental and emotional well being. During any crisis it is imperative to take care of our mental health as well as we do our physical health.

How is that possible? How do we make our emotional and mental health a priority?

When our kids are out of control, what is the parents response? You give them a "Time Out". Adults need a time out as well to manage emotional eruptions! There is no control as of yet for this pandemic/plague.What one can do is take control over their emotions.

So "Time-Out" RESET, get refocused. How does one do that? STOP, BREATHE, MEDITATE, RESET! *Finally, brethren, whatsoever things are true, whatsoever things are honest, whatsoever things are just, whatsoever things are pure, whatsoever things are lovely, whatsoever things are of good report; if there be any virtue, and if there be any praise, think on these things.* Philippians 4:8 (KJV).

The good news is we survived this far. We are not ill from this pandemic that has shaken the globe.

Sadden by those who have lost their lives and the mental anguish the families are facing because of it. Affected by job loss, and whatever other circumstances, if you are reading this you are still here and can reposition/adjust/alter the way we think and respond to a given situation.

- Take a step away from what is seen and not stay focused on what is. How am I allowing my behavior affecting those around me. Get rest, meditate. *This book of the law shall not depart out of thy mouth; but thou shalt meditate therein day and night, that thou mayest observe to do according to all that is written therein: for then thou shalt make thy way prosperous, and then thou shalt have good success.* Joshua 1:8 (KJV).
- Now is a good time to make use of writing-journal if you will. Express how, and what you are feeling and why. Clear your mind by doing that simple plan.
- What brings you joy? Somebody thought "shopping," rethink that, during this time. Spending time with your immediate family. Be creative.
- Limited social media, and newscasts.
- Got time? Call a friend whom you haven't spoken to in a while, call a family member you once were at odds with.
- Make new reachable, obtainable goals, not resolutions.
- Self talk, affirm/encourage yourself

There are many accounts in the bible where great kings, and great nations and prominent people become impaired with mental health conditions over a period of time. Life circumstances happen and these seemingly relentless circumstances rage war in the mind. When all seems hopeless, when one predicts that the human capacity to render a solution causes emotional helplessness, when GOD seems a far way off and no solutions has been given, fear and dread overtake this more likely can develop into depression.

Samuel was old, the people wanted to be *like all the nations* (1Samuel 8: 5) Authorized King James Version) demanding a king to judge them. Samuel was reminded that he was not the one the people rejected but God was who they rejected.Vs 7. The one chosen by God was Saul, son of Kish.Saul was described as *"a choice young man and a goodly"*: and *there was not among the children of Israel a "goodlier person as he": from his shoulders and upward he was higher than any of the people.* (1 Samuel 9: 2, 1Samuel 10:24, 1 Samuel 12:13)

Saul, from humble beginnings (1 Samuel 9:21) *Am not I a Benjamite, of the smallest of the tribes of Israel?and the least of all the families of the tribe of Benjamin?* (AKJV) was anointed, by Samuel, as king over Israel. Imagine the honor, prestige, and any other emotion that emerges with the great responsibility of governing over massive people. As time progressed Saul, because of the pressure and the demands of the people, foolishly disobeyed what God had commanded of him! 1 Samuel 13:6-14, 1 Samuel 15: 3-28) Results from exaltation to being abased. God had rejected Saul as king and rent/tore the kingdom of Israel from him. Saul, still reigned as king for a time, however no longer had the grace to fulfill his civic duty as king. Uncertain about the future and being mentally and emotionally derailed, (1 Samuel 16:14-16) Saul needed some resolution to his demise. What helped Saul's mental anguish-music, it soothed his soul and when the gifted and anointed son of Jesse played skillfully, Saul was mentally rejuvenated.

Saul diagnostically suffered (manic depressive) now deemed bipolar 1 disorder with manic episodes (I'm sure there may be some who may not agree, however DSM-5 backed by the American Psychiatric Association holds credence).

As a mental health therapist for adults (dual diagnosed), and a mental health child and adolescence for nearly a decade and having to have provisionally diagnosed each referred individual according to the diagnostic criteria from the DSM-5 and the American Psychiatric

Association.This author will safely state without diagnosing Saul's behavior, that Saul's behavior was indicative of a mental health condition.

Nebuchadnezzar, 2 Kings 24, 25; 2 Chronicles 36; Jeremiah 21-52; and (Daniel 4:4) *I Nebuchadnezzar was at rest in mine house, and flourishing in my palace: 5 I saw a dream which made me afraid, and the thoughts upon my bed and the visions of my head troubled me.*

His dream began to plague his mind and needed this dream interpreted. (Daniel 4:13-18) The interpretation was that his mental state would be disrupted for a period of time (Daniel 4:25)*That they shall drive thee from men, and thy dwelling shall be with the beasts of the field, and they shall make thee to eat grass as oxen, and they shall wet thee with the dew of heaven, and seven times shall pass over thee, till thou know that the most High ruleth in the kingdom of men, and giveth it to whomsoever he will.* This powerful king of Babylon was humbled by Almighty God.

Another biblical character to consider having been challenged with mental health decline. *David was **greatly distressed**; for the people spake of stoning him, because the soul of all the people was grieved, every man for his sons and for his daughters: **but David encouraged himself** in the LORD his God."* (1Samuel 30:6) If David did it...so can You. "I Am strong, I am an overcomer, I can do all things" Yes we/You/I can We can overcome this. In times of trouble and times of doubt, *I can do all this through him who gives me strength.* Philippians 4:13 (NIV) Other references Romans 8:16-17;37; 2 Corinthians 5:21; Deuteronomy 28:13. See how many ways you can find to **encourage yourself**.

Chapter Ten

NOW THAT WE KNOW, WHAT DO WE DO?

Think back, a year, two, more. I'm sure you can recall a friend, family member colleague, congregant who completed suicide. As painful as it may still be,take a moment and think where there any signs? If there were, did you know what to say or do?

True story: (Name has been changed to protect the innocent) I can recall an individual who in the past year or so, seemed oddly distrait to the here and now. This individual consistently had a blank stare on their face. I can not remember a time when this person smiled-ever. Even when folks were almost splitting their sides laughing at something someone said, the person was phlegmatic.

Granted, when this individual needed to fulfill any church duty, they were faithful in doing their part.

This individual was in a key leadership position, well liked, dutiful spouse, and parent, had insight into the lives of others and was prophetically intuitive. Week after week Keenan would perform church obligations and after service would fellowship briefly and excuse themself and exit the building.

Often Keenan would be sitting outside the church sitting, staring into space or smoking doing the same. Unless someone acknowledged him sitting there he would continue gazing off into the distance. It was uncertain as to how long, Keenan suffered in silence, yet it was obvious something was happening deep on the inside. Keenan's struggle was so intense he would end up disconnecting emotionally and mentally, unable to function in day-to-day living for quite some time. For at least a year there had been turmoil in the home. Not too many were privy to what was happening on the home front. After a while the entire family appeared joyless and dolorous. Did they seek counseling, possibly, no one was the wiser. The family tended to keep home matters discreet.

Weeks, months, possible years the family issues remained unresolved until one weekend major marital upheaval ripped through the Keenan's home between the spouses. Malicious, and spiteful words were exchanged.

Keenan made the threat of "killing himself", his spouse uttered "have at it." That day was a day that time seemed to have stood still. Keenan accepted the challenge. This loving husband, father, born again believer, a leader in the local church terminated his life.

Shock waves ripped through the family, the entire community, and the church family. Disbelief, and horror rocked everyone in his sphere of influence. Keenan had not responded to family members calling him for dinner. A family member searched the home to see why he had not responded. When they found him, what they witnessed was his limp and lifeless body. Attempts to resuscitate were unsuccessful, he was gone. His family, church family, co-workers were left confused, in pain, and deeply grieving.

He had previously confided to a close friend his feelings of not being the best he could be. The friend suggested he pray not sure what to say or to convince him to seek professional counseling.

Keenan's family, church family, was unprepared to effectively address mental health issues with him and seemingly neglected the obvious signs and symptoms. His employer was clueless as to anything out of the ordinary going on with him except he had been calling off quite frequently, complaining of blinding frequent headaches. Once the family began discussing his behavior and what they noticed.

The symptoms were there, Keenan suffered from depression. His family, and church family was unprepared to effectively address mental health issues with him nor knew how to respond to his condition. One way the family and his church family particularly could have better prepared was to understand these realities of mental illness assuredly exists among churches across this country.

The DSM-5 outlines the following specification to make a diagnosis of depression. The individual (Keenan) must have been experiencing **five** or more symptoms during the same 2-week period and at least one of the symptoms should be either (1) depressed mood or (2) loss of interest or pleasure.

Here were Keenan's symptoms:

1. Depressed mood most of the day, nearly every day.
2. Slowing down of his thoughts and physical movement (observable by family members and others, feeling restless).
3. Fatigue or lack of energy nearly every day.
4. Feeling worthless (which he had confided to a friend) also excessive and inappropriate guilt (feeling he didn't measure up as a husband, not sure if he is or can be a good father) nearly every day.

5. Difficulty thinking or concentrating, (frequently staring off into space) nearly every day.
6. Recurring thoughts of death, (better off dead) recurring suicidal ideation however he had no specific plan.

Now we know, what do we do moving forward to help others?

Do you think or know of someone you care about who may be suffering from depression? It is important to **know the warning signs** of suicide and to take suicidal statements extremely seriously.

LISTEN intently a person with suicidal ideation might say something like, "I'm going to kill myself," or other passive statements such as, "I wish I could just go to sleep and never wake up,"

Depressed individuals may present as irritabile, brooding, have obsessive thinking, complain of anxiety, have phobias, worry excessively over their physical health, or complain of pain.

In an earlier chapter there was a notation about depression Vs sadness and how they differ. Let's reiterate that: Note being sad because of the death of a loved one, termination of a relationship and bouts of sadness may not necessarily be depression.

Depression is more than just sadness. Sadness is a normal emotion and everyone at some point will experience it in his or her lifetime. A person who suffers from depression feels sad or hopeless about everything. This person may have every reason imaginable to be happy and yet lose the ability to experience joy or pleasure. Even though you may be sad for a few days, one still enjoys their favorite things.

Depression disrupts whatever is/was considered "normal" and that individual struggles to even get out of bed daily. People struggling with severe depression may entertain thoughts of self-harm, death, or suicide, or may have a suicide plan.

If you know of someone who shows signs or symptoms of depression encourage them to seek professional help. If you are worried about someone else, or just need emotional support, the emergency Lifeline network is available 24/7. You can call **1-800-273-8255** or go to Lifeline's website for a live chat.[1]

Here are a few responses that may be helpful to say to someone struggling with symptoms of depression and/or anxiety.

1. Share the positive points of your story. "I understand what you are going through, that happened to me a few years ago, I spoke to my doctor, they referred me to a therapist."
2. I am concerned about you.
3. Ask, "How long have you been feeling this way?"
4. Have you spoken to someone about this before/recently?"
5. Ask, "Is something bothering you?"
6. You haven't been joining/fellowshipping with us lately-are you ok?"
7. "It's difficult for me to understand what you are going through, but I can see you are distressed."
8. Something seems to be bothering you, Do you want to talk about it?"
9. "If what you have been experiencing has been present for a long time. I think it is important to see your family physician. I will be happy to go with you if you need me to."

Chapter Eleven

THAT CAN'T HAPPEN IN MY FAMILY, I'M (<u>FILL IN THE BLANK</u>).

Why is it that when *some* come to the conclusion that once we accept Christ into our lives everything will be a proverbial phrase "a bed of roses...smooth sailing, peaches and cream, perfecta/o?" That's so not scriptural. (**Job 14:1** *Man that is born of a woman is of few days and full of trouble;*

John 16:33 *These things I have spoken unto you, that in me ye might have peace. In the world ye shall have tribulation: but be of good cheer; I have overcome the world.*

2 Corinthians 4:8-9; 16-17; *We are troubled on every side, yet not distressed; we are perplexed, but not in despair; 9 Persecuted, but not forsaken; cast down, but not destroyed;*

16 For which cause we faint not; but though our outward man perishes, yet the inward man is renewed day by day.

17 For our light affliction, which is but for a moment, worketh for us a far more exceeding and eternal weight of glory)

It can happen in your/my family/even in the church

Job 1:1; 8-9; 18-19. *There was a man in the land of Uz, whose name was Job; and that man was* **perfect and upright,** *and one that feared God, and eschewed evil.*

8And the LORD said unto Satan, Hast thou considered my servant Job, that there is none like him in the earth, a perfect and an upright man, one that feareth God, and escheweth evil? 9Then Satan answered the LORD, and said, Doth Job fear God for nought? 18While he was yet speaking, there came also another, and said, Thy sons and thy daughters were eating and drinking wine in their eldest brother's house: (biblehub.com)

19 And, behold, there came a great wind from the wilderness, and smote the four corners of the house, and it fell upon the young men, and they are dead; (suffered loss of his children)

Job 2: *7 So went Satan forth from the presence of the LORD, and smote Job with sore boils from the sole of his foot unto his crown (illness)* (biblehub.com)

2 Kings 20:1-3 *In those days was Hezekiah(***a king who had a close relationship with God,*** *one who did "what was good and right and faithful before the Lord his God) ...* ***sick*** *unto death. And the prophet Isaiah the son of Amoz came to him, and said unto him, Thus saith the LORD, Set thine house in order; for thou shalt die, and not live. 2Then he turned his face to the wall, and prayed unto the LORD, saying, 3I beseech thee, O LORD, remember now how I have walked before thee in truth and with a perfect heart, and have done that which is good in thy sight. And Hezekiah wept sore.*

I could go on! **1Samuel 2:22, 25b** (Hophni and Phinehas) Their father (Eli) was **a Jewish priest** in the sanctuary of the Lord. *Now Eli was very old, and heard all that **his sons** did unto all Israel; and how they lay with the women that assembled at the door of the tabernacle of the congregation. Notwithstanding they hearkened not unto the voice of their father...*(unruly sons).

1 Samuel 31: 2-4 *And the Philistines followed hard upon Saul and upon his sons; and the Philistines slew Jonathan, and Abinadab, and Malchishua, Saul's sons. **3** And the battle went sore against Saul, and the archers hit him; and he was sore wounded by the archers. **4**Then said Saul unto his armour bearer, Draw thy sword, and thrust me through therewith; lest these uncircumcised come and thrust me through, and abuse me. But his armour bearer would not; for he was sore afraid. Therefore* (king*)* *Saul took a sword, and fell upon it.*_(**completed suicide**) (biblehub.com)

Psalm 42:5*Why art thou cast down, O my soul? and why art thou disquieted in me? hope thou in God: for I shall yet praise him for the help of his countenance.*, (depression)

Psalm 42:11*"Why art thou cast down, O my soul? and why art thou disquieted within me? hope thou in God: for I shall yet praise him, who is the health of my countenance, and my God."* (KJV) bible online

Matthew 17: 14, 15 *And when they were come to the multitude, there came to him a certain man, kneeling down to him, and saying, **15** Lord, have mercy on **my son:** for he is lunatick, and sore vexed: for ofttimes he falleth into the fire, and oft into the water.* (Son having a demon-healed) (biblehub.com)

- **Matthew 5: 10,11** *(persecuted for righteousness' sake)*
- **Matthew 5:43** *(despitefully use you)*
- **2 Corinthians 4: 8,9** *(We are **troubled on every side**, yet not distressed; we are perplexed, but not in despair; Persecuted, but not forsaken; cast down, but not destroyed)*

- **1 Peter 4: 12** (*.Beloved, think it not strange concerning the **fiery trial** which is to try you, as though some strange thing happened unto you*) KJV(biblegateway.com)

You say that's **back in bible times**...want something more current

April 6, 2013 – Megachurch **Pastor** Rick Warren (author of Purpose Driven Life) said Saturday that his 27-year-old son had commited suicide after a lifelong battle with mental illness. (abcnews.go.com)(fox news) Pastor Warren spoke of his son being incredibly kind, compassionate, and that his sweet spirit was a comfort to many. H states that the reason behind his youngest son's death was "Unfortunately, he also suffered from mental illness resulting in deep depression and suicidal thoughts." (huffpost.com)

Survey of black churches,what do these black pastors say...

SILENCE...

Chapter Twelve

ABOUT THE AUTHOR

Pittsburgh born native Preacher, teacher, prophetic voice to the local church she serves. Rev. Dr. Tammy is committed to serving God, and is affectionately known by her Christ Temple of Pittsburgh Church family, has a heart for equipping others to understand mental health and the challenges individuals face in various arenas, including faith based organizations.

Rev Dr. Tammy, a former Mental HealthFirst Aid (MHFA) trainer while employed at Pittsburgh Mercy has with her co-workers trained many adults in mental health first aid, training included Adult, Child and Adolescent, Military/Veterans, Enforcement/Public Safety/ Corrections, Clergy MHFA. These trainings involved staff from Pittsburgh PublicSchools, Faith Based organizations, Foster Care agencies, Technical Institutes, etc. So what IS mental health first aid? Many have the tendency to bypass the mental health part and direct their focus on the words first aid. We all have an understanding of first aid or at least what it may encompass. Let's explore. A first aid kit at the office may consist of a list of required components corresponding to the work related job hazards. For major injury or trauma: Scissors, gauze pads, tourniquet, mouth barrier,

- minor injury (such as a cut or scrape): Adhesive bandages, antiseptic spray, cold compress
- eyecare: Eyewash stations, refill solution
- employee Comfort: Cold relief, allergy relief, headache relief, antacids
- burn Care: Burn dressing, burn spray, burn cream

Whether at home, in our cars, granted our home and or car first aid kits will be slightly different and not as comprehensive as those needed in the workplace.

This kit may consist of a wide assortment of adhesive bandages of all sizes, burn cream, a cold pack, disposable thermometer, disposable gloves, aluminized rescue blanket, antibiotic ointment packets, gauze pads, sting relief wipes, ibuprofen, aspirin, and non-aspirin pills (this type of medication is used to temporarily treat symptoms caused by the common cold, flu, allergies, or other breathing illnesses (such as sinusitis, bronchitis). Decongestants help relieve stuffy nose, sinus, and ear congestion symptoms. Acetaminophen (APAP) is a non-aspirin pain reliever and fever reducer) covering things from headaches to cuts and burns.

Mental Health First Aid (MHFA) like first aid is the **initial** help given to an individual experiencing mental problems prior to proper/professional treatment needed or obtained.

When an individual comes across a person who has been injured and they appear unresponsive, as a first responder (not an EMT) but a "good samaritan" the first response according to American Red Cross' CPR and First Aid[1]

Check the scene for the safety of you and the victim. Tap and shout "are you ok" to ensure that person needs help. Check for vital signs. If that person is in need of help, Call 911 for assistance and begin administering assistance. Open the airway. With the person lying on his or her back, tilt the head back slightly to lift the chin.

Check for breathing. Listen carefully, for no more than 10 seconds, for sounds of breathing. If there is no breathing begin CPR. Placing your hands, one on top of the other, in the middle of the individual's chest pushing hard and pushing fast, using your body weight to help you with compressions that are at least 2 inches deep and administered at a rate of at least 100 compressions per minute.

Deliver rescue breaths. With the person's head tilted back slightly and the chin lifted, pinch the nose closed and place your mouth (using some covering i.e. handkerchief of cloth) over the person's mouth to make a complete seal. Blow into the person's mouth to make the chest rise. Delivering two rescue breaths, then continuing compressions.

Continue CPR steps.

Keep performing cycles of chest compressions and breathing until the person exhibits signs of life, such as breathing, an AED becomes available, or EMS or a trained medical responder arrives on scene. Mental Health First Aid like CPR is giving the initial help offered to an individual who is or maybe experiencing a mental health crisis.[2]

Training MHFA to individuals is to eradicate the stigma associated with mental illness and to heighten the awareness of the signs and symptoms, to teach how to provide that initial help and how to appropriately direct the individual experiencing mental illness to the proper professionals when necessary. When individuals are trained in mental health first aid (not as professionals or having the ability to make diagnoses) but it will help those to be aware that mental health problems are common as mentioned in an earlier chapter, reduce any fear and stigma associated with it, be informed of how, if and when to respond. MHFA training will help to increase skills and one's confidence in becoming a help to their family, friends, community, and above all their churches.

When facilitating the training, trainers specifically ask each participant what they hope to learn from the MHFA course and how they will use what they have learned in order to help others.

The training gives the definition of what mental health is, identifies mental health problems, that these problems are common, how mental health problems impact families, communities, cities, the individual that can cause disability throughout the individuals life. The course defines disorders i.e. depression, anxiety, psychosis substance use and eating disorders.

To help the participants how to respond in a mental health crisis including, just to name a few-suicidal thoughts and behaviors, first aid for self injury, first aid for aggressive behavior. The course also gives reference to the types of therapies that have been developed for treatment.

As a mental health therapist for dual diagnosed adults and a mental health child and adolescent therapist for nearly a decade and having to have provisionally diagnosed each referred individual according to the diagnostic criteria from the DSM-5 and the American Psychiatric Association. I have witnessed the mental anguish of the individuals coming to seek a remedy to their pain.

This author early on saw individuals from all walks of life having been affected by mental illness resulting from various life experiences i.e. drug addiction, medication use and abuse, personal assault and the list goes on.

In the midst of a storm

How has this author been able to handle her own pain without having experienced the full extent of mental problems? We all have experienced at one point in our lives, anxiety, or even some sadness (short of depression) having faced life experiences. It was how the author determined to be a victor and not a victim mentality. As the reader may recall the definition of depression: being **sad** because of the death of a loved one, termination of a relationship and bouts of sadness may not necessarily be depression. That depression *causes feelings of sadness, a loss of interest in activities once enjoyed. It can lead to various emotional and physical problems decreasing a person's ability to function at work and at home.*

Anxiety: fearful feelings that can cause dread, tension, resulting in physical manifestations, headaches, body aches and pain, impulsive behavior-overeating, resulting in weight gain,or lack of eating which can cause weight loss, or some other form of illness-hypertension etc.

Had this author experienced any of the above mentioned. Yes. Job related-indeed. It is normal to experience some stress from one's job. When you don't adequately process that stress and allow that pressure to build up (speaking from personal experience) physical problems can and will occur. One can find themselves having to call and make an appointment with their primary physician.

Not everyone will experience the same symptoms as being described. What the author is sharing is her own personal experience, signs, and symptoms she experienced from the onset of anxiety. Because of unexplained headaches, spasms in the eye and chest pain it was time to seek professional help.

Having done so this author's PCP explained that the symptoms of chest pains, constant twitching in the eye, frequent headaches were caused by anxiety.

As the physician began to ask a series of questions the diagnosis rang true. The physician ordered tests to rule any major problems or any brain injuries.

Test results are all negative. The physician went on to prescribe med-i-ca-tion for anxiety. It was then, having left the physician's office,medication in hand, that became the pivotal point for this author to resist what was emotionally being **permitted** to the point of an overwhelming response that the author **can control**. This author had allowed what she was experiencing from the job, from "life", from what others had said and done on the job, at home, from *church* to continuously run a muck in her head. Determined to resolve the issues that was being permitted to plague the mind, will, and emotions, it was high time to put away the "stickin" thinking realizing one can not control the behaviors of others, however one can control how to respond appropriately to the given situation without it negatively impacting your environment and or emotional space. The occupation at that time where the author was employed ended by the authors choice.What did transpire was the fulfillment of being able to help others who may be struggling within themselves emotionally. The author developed and implemented a support services program, became involved in a community program that helped individuals struggling with mental health challenges as well substance use. This process began several decades of assisting others through their journey to become emotionally and mentally healthy to recover from life challenges, rebuild relationships and fulfill God's plan and purpose for their lives.

The journey begins

This author having graduated from Penn State University with a Masters in Counselor Education with a Chemical Dependency emphasis became involved in a community program to help provide support services to men and their families having transitioned from years of drug addiction, incarceration to a halfway house and with the hope of returning to their respective family members.

This author has witnessed many of these consumers' lives changed and the reward of services provided seen these individuals turn their lives around, one started an eatery, another has a successful line of hair growth products, another currently is a peer specialist sharing a story of recovery.

The author continued the journey by facilitating a support services program of her own (non-profit), while continuing to provide services as an adult mental health therapist serving individuals with mental health challenges and substance use disorder (comorbidity).

Comorbidity as the author understands it is defined as when an individual has more than one disorder at the same time.

It could be (as some of my clients were diagnosed as dual diagnosed) **common** mental health disorders accompanied with substance use disorders (mental health disorder and addiction) as one example among many.

Comorbidity/comorbidity disorder and addiction; mental health comorbidity -two mental health disorders coexisting at the same time in one individual/person.

What do the experts say:

According to the National Association on Mental Illness (NAMI) direct quote: *Substance use disorders — the repeated misuse of alcohol and/or drugs — often occur simultaneously in individuals with mental illness, usually to cope with overwhelming symptoms. The combination of these two illnesses has its own term: dual diagnosis, or co-occurring disorders. Either disorder (substance use or mental illness) can develop first.*

*According to the National Survey on Drug Use and Health, **9.2 million** U.S. adults experienced both mental illness and a substance use disorder in **2018**.*[3]

~~Having~~ come to the very edge of developing an anxiety disorder and having experienced an anxiety attack two decades before. It was a time when I was teaching preschool for an organization (remaining nameless, those who know me know who I was working for at that time). It was on a Friday and the facility where our center was located was in a church basement.The church had bingo on Friday's and all our preschool equipment had to be put away and stored in a space no larger than a 5'x7' room or smaller. Prior to that as the teacher I had to ensure that the next week's lesson plan was completed and ready to turn into the Education Supervisor before the end of the day. My assistant and I had just completed that and it was less than 2 hours before quitting time and we still needed to pack up the entire room: bookshelves, play unit, rocking chair, area rug, bikes,wagons, work table, sand and water table, just to name a few items.

We also had to drive to the central office to drop off the lesson plans. Stressed for lack of time and other obligations, and inside that small space trying to make everything fit...the onset of an anxiety attack occurred. Not knowing what was happening and not aware of what was happening to an over exerted body, consciousness was fading quickly. Calling out for help to another stressed individual not aware that the LAST thing you do is hand someone a brown paper bag to breathe in while having a panic attack and not trained in CPR, could prove fatal. Taking the brown bag away from the face and calming the breathing helped and not becoming fully unconscious this author was able to regroup from what had just occurred remained a mystery UNTIL being trained as a MentalHealth First Aid participant and then instructor.

This author now knows what she had experienced and the proper procedure in responding to an individual experiencing a panic attack.

Years later, newly married and having relocated to an unfamiliar area the journey begins again. Knowing what it is like to be so stressed and overwhelmed with an unfaithful partner, school stress, financial stress and trying to parent at a distance. The pain of it all, from the stress began to deteriorate my physical body, kidneys were inflamed causing me to end up in the emergency room in Dayton Ohio and my mind telling me I was never going to leave that hospital alive bleeding internally. Most who have had the experience of waiting to be seen in the ER seems like an eternity and the battle rages on in one's mind. Every emotion imaginable presents itself front and center. You become afraid,every time you use the restroom and each time the water is not a tinge of yellow but deep red yes (blood). Of course when you witness that you have a tendency to forget who's and who you are (a child of God) and the authority dwelling within you. Being afraid works its way to fear (fear it torment)...1 John 4:18... or 2 Timothy 1:7 For God hath not given us the spirit of fear; but of power, love, and a sound mind. OH COURSE that sounds all well and good, however when you are in the ***midst of the storm,*** all that word and bible teaching and preaching goes swooping right out of your befuddled mind. This author has been and is able to empathize with those who struggle with mental health challenges.

This led to a career of helping others, witnessing their pain and offering services and resources to help them gain a healthy lifestyle emotionally and mentally. Having established professional relationships and building trust with the clients the author's clients began to share their stories of what they used to be and what they were at that moment in time.

One by one, male and female became transparent with this unfamiliar person as they disclosed the pain inside without being judged, without being ridiculed, without being ashamed or feeling as though they had to justify being in the condition they are/were currently.

Most clients are not looking for advice or to hear a person say "If I were you", simply because you are not them!

You are not experiencing the emotional and mental anguish they are dealing with at that given moment.

What they are looking for is an individual who has an empathetic and who has an intensely listening ear and will help them decipher their current status and help them effectively process the situation and begin a mentally healthy lifestyle. The attendee stemmed from all walks of life from prestigious individuals to everyday people such as you and the author of this book. No one is exempt and as John Bradford coined the phrase/proverb… "but for the grace of God there go I"[4] His reference was in regards to a group of prisoners being led to an execution, which could have been his fate. John Bradford was to have paraphrased the verse the Apostle Paul wrote about in the bible **1 Corinthians 15: 8-10** and it reads from the KJV: **8** And last of all he was seen of me also, as of one born out of due time.**9** For I am the least of the apostles, that am not meet to be called an apostle, because I persecuted the church of God.**10** But by the grace of God I am what I am: and his grace which was bestowed upon me was not in vain; but I laboured more abundantly than they all: yet not I, but the grace of God which was with me.[5] When you think about it, those struggling with a mental illness can be considered imprisoned in their minds having lost hope of their present situation ever improving and with those thoughts become disable emotionally having difficulty functioning at work, school, and in daily life.

As an individual first and as a mental health therapist for adults I concur with that statement and having teetered on the brink of mental illness I can truly say "There for the grace of God…"

Some of the clients treated began to share childhood difficulties causing the author's curiosity to peek and sparked an interest in treating children and adolescents.

As a position opened for intervention/prevention-school based another path taken to help students manage behavior and to assist education staff better manage unwanted behavior in the classroom.

This was done by providing lessons on what acceptable behavior is expected and activities that coincided with the lessons the adults involved began to grasp the concept that kids have problems too.

As a School Based Therapist providing services to students K-12. A typical caseload depending on the school assigned to, would reach 26 + students. In consulting with parents it was difficult for most to comprehend that kids, not just theirs, other children as well experience mental health problems just as adults do. Having trained education staff in MentalHealth First Aid helped them to understand but not diagnose child and adolescent behavior in a whole new light thus helping students get the initial help they need.

Mental Health First Aid for Youth similar in nature to adult mental health first aid. It is help offered to a young person who is experiencing mental health challenges, disorder, or a mental health crisis.[2]

There is a slight variation regarding adult mental health first aid versus youth mental health first aid, in that youth may experience mental health problems differently. Youth are less informed regarding mental health. As with adults, youth with mental health problems are often misunderstood and discriminated against. More often than not youth tend to be ostracized by their peers, less tolerated by school adults and sometimes parents who are unaware of the problem. As a school based therapist I again have witnessed the pain associated with mental health challenges in youth, the frustration they feel (based on heir disclosure during sessions) when their peers ridicule them, disassociate with them, harsh words from school staff who do not total understand the reality of any given student experiencing mental understand mental health problems.

The author often had to console the parents who did/does not understand mental health problems and would say in so many words ":fix my kid so they will be good in school and at home."

Several students' preliminary diagnosis ranged from Anxiety Disorder, ADHD/ADD (in younger kids), Disruptive Mood Dysregulation, Separation Anxiety, Trauma and Stressor-related Disorder, and Adjustment Disorder-experienced from parents separating and moving to a new location. In working with these students over the years there have been many rewards. Parents and staff report that they have witnessed significant changes in behavior.

The best yet a student (Separation Anxiety) has adjusted well to therapy as is being referred to the schools gifted program. Having Trained as both Adult and Youth Mental Health Instructor this author was able to utilize skills obtained and to put into practice those skills while interacting with adults and youth alike.

Rev Dr. Tammy is also CEO/Founder of Bear International BGAP Inc family support services for families recovering from life's challenges,

During the years of being at Hilltop and Parkview Manor community resources were made available through the collaboration of Bear International BGAP Inc and agencies, i.e. **Allegheny Health Department** during a holistic health fair providing dental cleaning to children and adults and other health resources made available through AHD.

Other organizations came and spoke to women's health, domestic violence, parenting skills. Families were provided produce from **Greater Pittsburgh Food Bank.** The afterschool and summer camp "Kidz View" that operated out of Duquesne, Pa-Hilltop and Parkvue Manor housing complex provided games, educational activities, help with homework, and also provided meals and snacks sponsored by GPFB and Summer Foods".

Highmark High Five program provided an activities program manual to help prevent childhood obesity. Bear International BGAP Inc in collaboration with **Tickets for Kids** provided educational experiences via field trips to Hartwood Acres, Festival of Lights. The fifty plus children who attended Kidz View were given an opportunity to participate in a holiday event "It's not all about me" where items were purchased and distributed to the residence of an area nursing home during Christmas time. Kids and adults sang Christmas carols together; it was an amazing time and learning experience of giving. until the women's ministry "Fresh Wind" pulled her away.

A few words regarding Fresh Wind-women's ministry. Rev Dr,Tammy has again utilized the skill set obtained from the years of experience as a therapist and mental health instructor to understand the significance and importance of self care. From that realization Fresh Wind was born and women from all walks of life participated in the quarterly "Spa Days" held at her residence. Massage therapists, massage chairs,aroma therapy and various healing stations were set up to "minister" to women who were either overwhelmed from the many responsibilities women in general face on a daily basis (wife, mother, caregiver, employee, chief cook, and bottle washer just to name a few. It was a time for women to come together and get a "fresh wind" and new perspective on life's responsibilities, to relax and recuperate, reboot and be ready to face challenges head on minus the anxiety. Rev Dr. Tammy at some point hopes to resurrect "Fresh Wind" when the pandemic has subsided significantly where face masks and social distancing and occupancy limitations have lifted. We all could use a "Spa Day" to reset and forge ahead to the next phase that life and the church has.

God has transitioned Rev Tammy from Florida, back to Pa. Having answered a clarion call and hearing the sound of a shofar blowing one evening. Returning to Pittsburgh she has been faithful in serving under the illustrious Pastor Marvin and First Lady Sheila Edwell-Rawlings who she has submitted her life, ministry, and accountability to. She currently serves as pastoral director of Christian Education and Sunday School department, and prophetic ministry at Christ Temple Church of Pgh.

Because of the devastation this pandemic has caused and its impact on lives across this nation and because of the churches need for reformation inspired the author to compile this book to be a help and reference point specifically to the black church, however to every believer and church affiliation who has yet to embrace the reality of mental health problems and be prepared to "let the church be the church" and be a place of healing and restoration it once was.

References

Chapter **One** What Is mental illness?

1   Steve Austin (former pastor "I almost died")
2   National Alliance on Mental Illness (NAMI) 2
3   World Health Organization (WHO) 3
4   Mental Health.gov 4
5   Merriam Webster 5
6   American Psychiatric Association (July 2018)
7   Mayo Clinic 1

Chapter **Two** Types of mental illness

1   American Psychiatric Association
2   Mayo Clinic
3   Healthline
4   National Institute of Mental Health

Chapter **Three** Who's at risk?

1   World Health Organization (WHO) 3

Chapter **Four** Test your knowledge

1   Mental health America (screening)
2   MentalhealthFirstAid.org

Chapter **Five** Warning Signs We Overlooked

1   Mayo Clinic
2   Psychiatry Today
3   WebMD
4   Biblegateway.com and Biblehub.com

Chapter **Six** Statistically Speaking

1　American Psychiatric Asso. July 2018
2　Steve Austin

Chapter **Seven** Is it in our church? Yes

1　Time Magazine 7
2　Chrisitan Post (2019)
3　Steve Austin 7
4　Alicia Montgomery (NAMI article) 8

Chapter **Eight** Time to End the Silence

1　American Foundation of Suicide Prevention
2　Lifeway Research (erroneous thinking)

Chapter **Nine** Shore up Emotional and Mental Health

1　Biblegateway.com
2　Biblehub.com

Chapter **Ten** Now that we know, what do we do?

1　APA on DSM-5

Chapter **Eleven** That can't happen to me I'm_____

1　Biblegateway.com
2　Huffpost.com
3　Biblehub.com
4　(abcnews.go.com)
5　(fox news)

Chapter **Twelve**

1　American Red Cross
2　MentalHealth First Aid Association of Maryland, Missouri Dept. of Mental Health, and National Council for BehavioralHealth
3　National Association on Mental Illness (NAMI) *direct quote*
4　John Bradford on Wiktionary.org Phraphased 1 Corinthians 15:8-10
5　Biblegateway.com (KJV) 1 Corinthians 15: 8-10

Printed in the United States
By Bookmasters